STUDY GUIDE

The New Testament Canon

Michael J. Kruger

LIGONIER MINISTRIES

Renew your Mind.

LIGONIER.ORG | 800-435-4343

Contents

Introduction

Opponents of Christianity raise challenging questions about the origins, authorship, age, and reliability of the twenty-seven books of the New Testament. When the authenticity of the New Testament is questioned, so is the gospel. In this series, Dr. Michael J. Kruger critiques the most common objections to the canonicity of the New Testament and articulates sound reasons to believe with confidence that the New Testament is the authentic, true, and inspired Word of God.

This study guide is a companion to the video teaching series. Whether you are using the DVDs, streaming the videos on Ligonier.org, or going through the course in Ligonier Connect, this resource is designed to help you make the most of the learning experience. For each message in the series, there is a corresponding lesson in this guide. Here is what you will find in each lesson:

INTRODUCTION	The introduction is a brief paragraph that summarizes the content covered in the lecture and considered in the study guide lesson.
	How to use: Use the introduction to each lesson to get a sense of the big picture before watching the video. Refer to these statements as you work through the study guide to remind you of what you have already covered and where you are headed.
LEARNING GOALS	The learning goals are the knowledge and skills the study guide lesson will endeavor to equip you with as you work through the lecture content.
	How to use: Familiarize yourself with the goals of each lesson before engaging with its contents. Keeping the overall purpose in mind as you watch each video and reflect on or discuss the questions will help you get the most out of each lesson.
KEY IDEAS	The key ideas are the major points or takeaways from the lecture.
	How to use: Use these ideas to prepare yourself for each lesson and to review previous lessons. They describe specifically the knowledge each lecture is communicating.

REFLECTION & DISCUSSION QUESTIONS	The questions are the guided reflection and/or discussion component of the lesson that are intended to help you prepare for, process, and organize what you are learning.
	How to use: Reflect on individually or discuss in a group the questions in the order in which they appear in the lesson. The timestamps in the right margin indicate where the answers to questions during the video can be found.
PRAYER	The prayer section offers suggestions for how to close the lesson in prayer with respect to what was taught in the lecture.
	How to use: Consider using each lesson's prayer section as a guide to personal or group prayer. These sections follow the ACTS prayer model, which you can learn more about in R.C. Sproul's Crucial Questions booklet *Does Prayer Change Things?* This helpful guide is available as a free e-book at Ligonier.org.
REVIEW QUIZ	The review quiz is a set of six multiple-choice questions that appears at the end of each lesson.
	How to use: Use each quiz to check your comprehension and memory of the major points covered in each lecture. It will be most beneficial to your learning if you take a lesson's quiz either sometime between lessons or just before you begin the next lesson in the study guide.
ANSWER KEY	The answer key provides explanations for the reflection and discussion questions and answers to the multiple-choice questions in the review quiz.
	How to use: Use the answer key to check your own answers or when you do not know the answer. Note: Do not give in too quickly; struggling for a few moments to recall an answer reinforces it in your mind.

Study Schedules

The following table suggests four plans for working through *The New Testament Canon* video teaching series and this companion study guide. Whether you are going through this series on your own or with a group, these schedules should help you plan your study path.

	Extended 8-Week Plan	Standard 6-Week Plan	Abbreviated 4-Week Plan	Intensive 3-Week Plan
Week	Lesson			
1	*	1	1	1 & 2
2	1	2	2 & 3	3 & 4
3	2	3	4 & 5	5 & 6
4	3	4	6	
5	4	5		
6	5	6		
7	6			
8	*			

* For these weeks, rather than completing lessons, spend your time discussing and praying about your learning goals for the study (the first week) and the most valuable takeaways from the study (the last week).

1

The Problem of Canon

INTRODUCTION

Opponents of Christianity are launching bold new attacks against the foundation of Christian belief: the twenty-seven books of the New Testament. Directed at the average person and calculated to undermine confidence in the Bible, these popular and destructive ideas about the origins of the New Testament have gained a widespread audience. In this lecture, Dr. Kruger describes these contemporary challenges to Christian belief and explains why Christians cannot afford to allow these challenges to go unanswered.

LEARNING GOALS

When you have finished this lesson, you should be able to:

- Describe the problem of canon and explain its significance
- Identify three ongoing factors that contribute to the problem of canon

KEY IDEAS

- Contemporary attacks against the nature and reliability of the New Testament are focused at persuading ordinary Christians and are not going away.
- Christians need to be able to articulate the reasons they have confidence in the New Testament.
- Skepticism over the canon of the New Testament has been fueled primarily by doubts about authorship, discoveries of previously unknown writings, and the thesis that early Christianity was theologically diverse.

REFLECTION & DISCUSSION QUESTIONS

Before the Video

What Do You Think?

Take a moment to answer the following questions. They will prepare you for the lecture.

- What assumptions about the nature of the New Testament are common in our culture?

- Do challenges to the New Testament pose a serious threat to the credibility of the Christian faith? Explain your answer.

Scripture Reading

All Scripture is breathed out by God and profitable for teaching, for reproof, for correction, and for training in righteousness, that the man of God may be complete, equipped for every good work.

—2 Timothy 3:16–17

- What does this passage reveal about the origin and intent of the New Testament?

During the Video

Answer the following questions while you watch the video. They will guide you through the lecture.

Doubts about Authorship   *0:00–12:58*

- Why does the topic of canon appeal to critical scholars who want to discredit Christianity? CHRISTIANS DON'T HAVE THE ANSWERS ... TO EXTRA BOOKS...

FORGED (Book)
- What is the deeper challenge posed by the claims that critical scholars make about New Testament authorship?
  1- # OF DOUBTS RAISED OF THE AUTHORSHIP OF DIFFERENT BOOKS (FORGERIES)
  2- DISCOVERY OF MORE AND MORE (HIDDEN) BOOKS... ARCHEALOGICAL FINDS. (MORE TO COME)
  3- THE INFLUENCE OF WALTER BAUR... THAT EARLY CHRISTIANITY WAS THEOLOGICALLY DIVERSE.

New Discoveries → EACH GROUPS HAD THEIR OWN BOOKS. (no AGREEMENTS)   *12:58–18:23*

- Why is the lost city of Oxyrhynchus significant to the study of ancient documents? MANY OLD MANUSCRIPTS FOUND HERE (#2) ↑CLAIM

- What are the names of some of the noncanonical "gospels" that have been discovered?

  THOMAS , JESUS' WIFE , JUDAS

Bauer's Thesis   *18:23–22:30*

- What was Walter Bauer's central thesis? Why is it significant?

  EACH OF THE CHRISTIANITIES GROUPS HAD THEIR OWN SET OF BOOKS.

After the Video

Answer the following questions after you have finished the lecture. They will help you identify and summarize the major points.

- What is the problem of canon? Why does this represent a challenge to Christian belief?

  If you are in a group, have the members discuss factors that have made it challenging for them or for people they know to believe the Bible.

- How does Dr. Kruger respond to the suggestion that Christians should simply ignore the claims of critical scholars and focus on the Bible?

  If you are in a group, have the members discuss ways that Christians can prepare themselves to respond to the rapid spread of critical scholarship in mainstream culture.

- In your opinion, which of the three "tributaries" mentioned in this lecture poses the greatest challenge to Christianity? Which of these tributaries is easiest to respond to?

  If you are in a group, have the members identify the "tributary" that they consider to be most influential. How have you seen these ideas expressed in the news or in popular culture?

PRAYER

Commit what you have learned in this lesson to prayer.

- Praise God for recording His perfect and inerrant Word in the New Testament.
- Confess any doubts you may have about the trustworthiness of the New Testament.

- Thank God for His sovereign preservation of the New Testament over the centuries.
- Ask God to answer any difficult questions you have about the New Testament canon.

REVIEW QUIZ

Use these multiple-choice questions to measure what you learned from this lesson.

1. How many distinct ancient writings were contained in the codices discovered at Nag Hammadi, Egypt?
   a. 13
   b. 30
   c. 52
   d. 77

2. According to the Gospel of Thomas, salvation is found through which of the following?
   a. Faith alone
   b. Animal sacrifice
   c. Higher knowledge
   d. Righteous works

3. What does the term *apocryphal* mean?
   a. Counterfeit
   b. Forbidden
   c. Heretical
   d. Hidden

4. Accounts of the life of Jesus have been found that claim to have been written by all of the following *except*:
   a. Judas
   b. Paul
   c. Peter
   d. Thomas

5. Who wrote a book titled *Orthodoxy and Heresy in Earliest Christianity*?
   a. Karl Barth
   b. Bart Ehrman
   c. Bruce Metzger
   d. Walter Bauer   1a34   1471 =ENGLISH

6. What is ultimately at stake in contemporary debates about the New Testament canon?
   a. The intellectual credibility of Christian scholars
   b. Our access to new archaeological discoveries
   c. Our religious freedom
   d. The gospel

Answer Key—The Problem of Canon

Before the Video

What Do You Think?

These are personal questions. The answers should be based on your own knowledge and experience.

Scripture Reading

- What does this passage reveal about the origin and intent of the New Testament?

  This passage reveals that the origin of all Scripture, including the New Testament, is God Himself. God has graciously revealed Himself in His Word, and it is "profitable for teaching, for reproof, for correction, and for training in righteousness." God's ultimate purpose for breathing out these inspired words is that His people will be "complete, equipped for every good work."

During the Video

Doubts about Authorship

- Why does the topic of canon appeal to critical scholars who want to discredit Christianity?

  Critical scholars believe that most Christians are not prepared to answer questions about why certain ancient writings belong in the Bible and others do not. They suggest that all of these ancient writings are equally reliable and that it is a blind leap of faith to claim that the twenty-seven books of the New Testament are uniquely authored by God. By labeling this topic the "Achilles' heel of Christianity," critical scholars hope to discredit the Christian faith by undermining confidence in the New Testament.

- What is the deeper challenge posed by the claims that critical scholars make about New Testament authorship?

  Critical scholars do not merely raise questions about our ability to know who the authors of the New Testament are. They take this challenge a step further by suggesting that the authors intended to deceive their readers by falsely claiming to be Apostolic figures like Peter and Paul. These critical theories imply that the books of the New Testament are simply elaborate forgeries, unworthy of the trust that Christians place in them.

New Discoveries

- Why is the lost city of Oxyrhynchus significant to the study of ancient documents?

  The lost city of Oxyrhynchus is a significant archaeological site that was discovered in the late nineteenth century. Excavations in this city have revealed a wealth of ancient manuscripts. Many of the extracanonical books that fascinate critical scholars were discovered in the garbage heap at Oxyrhynchus.

- What are the names of some of the noncanonical "gospels" that have been discovered?

  A variety of extracanonical books have been discovered that claim to be gospels— that is, accounts of the life of Jesus. These writings include the Gospel of Thomas, the Gospel of Peter, the Gospel of Mary, and the Gospel of Judas. Unlike the four Gospels of the New Testament, these books are all forgeries, written long after the deaths of their alleged authors.

Bauer's Thesis

- What was Walter Bauer's central thesis? Why is it significant?

  In 1934, the German scholar Walter Bauer argued that early Christianity was theologically diverse, encompassing a broad array of views about Christology, the nature of God, and the meaning of salvation. This thesis is significant because it implies that traditional Christianity is merely one of many ancient forms of Christianity. Modern critical scholarship has embraced this thesis and used it to argue that all of the ancient Christian texts—canonical and extracanonical—speak with equal authority.

After the Video

- What is the problem of canon? Why does this represent a challenge to Christian belief?

  The problem of canon refers to the burden imposed on Christians by contemporary critical scholarship to explain why certain ancient writings are considered part of the canon of God's Word and other ancient writings are not. The problem of canon is expressed most simply in the question, "How can we know which books belong in the New Testament?" If the New Testament, as a foundation of Christian belief, is questioned, so is Christian belief itself.

- How does Dr. Kruger respond to the suggestion that Christians should simply ignore the claims of critical scholars and focus on the Bible?

  While it may be tempting simply to ignore such claims, Dr. Kruger states that Christians no longer have this luxury. Critical scholars intentionally market their ideas to laypeople in the form of popular-level books and articles. These challenges are not going to go away, and Christians who are not armed with answers to these questions are in danger of losing confidence in God's Word.

- In your opinion, which of the three "tributaries" mentioned in this lecture poses the greatest challenge to Christianity? Which of these tributaries is easiest to respond to?

  In this lecture, Dr. Kruger identifies three distinct factors that function as tributaries that feed the growing river of skepticism about the New Testament canon. These tributaries are doubts about the authorship of New Testament books, the increasing discoveries of extracanonical writings that claim to be gospels or epistles, and Bauer's thesis that ancient Christianity lacked a clear doctrinal and canonical consensus. Opinions about which of these factors represents the greatest challenge will vary.

REVIEW QUIZ

Lesson 1

1. **C.**

   The collection of ancient manuscripts uncovered at Nag Hammadi included thirteen codices, which collectively held a total of fifty-two individual writings.

2. **C.**

   The Gospel of Thomas articulates a view of salvation that is radically different from the gospel message of the New Testament. According to the Gospel of Thomas, salvation is obtained through higher knowledge. The author of this ancient text claims that we can save ourselves by gaining and mastering such knowledge.

3. **D.**

   The term apocryphal *means "hidden." To describe an ancient writing as* apocryphal *is to note that it appears to be similar to books of the Bible but is not considered part of the canon of Scripture.*

4. **B.**

   Various apocryphal gospels have been discovered that claim to have been written by Judas, Mary Magdalene, Peter, Philip, Thomas, and many others. However, an apocryphal "Gospel of Paul" has yet to be found.

5. **D.**

   German scholar Walter Bauer wrote Orthodoxy and Heresy in Earliest Christianity *in 1934. Translated into English in the 1970s, this book has profoundly influenced contemporary critical scholarship.*

6. **D.**

   The very gospel that Christians preach, teach, and believe is at stake. If Christians cannot respond to the challenges of contemporary critical scholarship, then we cannot credibly claim to have a coherent New Testament. If there is no coherent New Testament, then there cannot be a coherent New Testament message. The gospel message would lose the foundation on which it stands.

2

The Definition of Canon

INTRODUCTION

Our understanding of when and how the New Testament canon came about is profoundly shaped by our perception of what canon is. In this lecture, Dr. Kruger describes three distinct ways of defining canon and explains how each of these definitions points us toward an important aspect of how God gave His Word to His church.

LEARNING GOALS

When you have finished this lesson, you should be able to:

- Identify and explain three distinct definitions of canon
- Describe how the definitions of canon fit together to present a fuller picture of the process of canonicity

KEY IDEAS

- The way that the canon is defined determines the way that the canon is dated.
- The exclusive, functional, and ontological definitions of canon are three helpful and complementary ways to define what the canon is.
- The definitions of canon show that the development of the canon was a multi-stage process instead of a one-time event.

REFLECTION & DISCUSSION QUESTIONS

Before the Video

What Do You Think?

Take a moment to answer the following questions. They will prepare you for the lecture.

- What requirements does a book need to meet in order to be considered part of the biblical canon?

- Who has the right to decide whether a specific book belongs in the Bible? Why?

Scripture Reading

I warn everyone who hears the words of the prophecy of this book: if anyone adds to them, God will add to him the plagues described in this book, and if anyone takes away from the words of the book of this prophecy, God will take away his share in the tree of life and in the holy city, which are described in this book.

—Revelation 22:18–19

- What do these verses teach about the sacred nature of God's inspired words?

During the Video

Answer the following questions while you watch the video. They will guide you through the lecture.

The Exclusive Definition of Canon   0:00–12:43

- According to the exclusive definition of canon, what determines the canonical status of a book?

- How does holding the exclusive definition of canon affect the date that one assigns to the canon?

The Functional Definition of Canon   12:43–19:04

- According to the functional definition of canon, what determines the canonical status of a book?

- How does holding the functional definition of canon affect the date that one assigns to the canon?

The Ontological Definition of Canon   19:04–23:21

- According to the ontological definition of canon, what determines the canonical status of a book?

- How does holding the ontological definition of canon affect the date that one assigns to the canon?

After the Video

Answer the following questions after you have finished the lecture. They will help you identify and summarize the major points.

- Does an understanding of history lead to a definition of canon, or does a definition of canon lead to a particular understanding of history? Explain your answer.

  If you are in a group, have the members share what impressions, if any, about the development of canon they have held in the past. How has this lecture changed your perception about the canon's development?

- What are the strengths and weaknesses of each of the three definitions of canon?

  If you are in a group, have the members identify which of these definitions is most helpful to their understanding of the canon and why.

- What is the big picture of the canon's development that these three definitions form when considered together?

  If you are in a group, have the members discuss their confidence in the reliability of the canon based on this fuller picture of its development.

PRAYER

Commit what you have learned in this lesson to prayer.

- Praise God for giving us a complete canon of sixty-six Old and New Testament books.
- Confess ways in which you struggle to integrate God's Word into your daily life.
- Thank God for speaking through His Word to believers centuries ago and to you today.
- Ask God to help you to develop a closer relationship with Him through His Word.

REVIEW QUIZ

Use these multiple-choice questions to measure what you learned from this lesson.

1. Which of the following best describes the church's role in the formation of the canon?
   a. The church created the canon.
   b. The church operated without a canon until the fourth century.
   c. The church debated the canonical status of certain books for centuries.
   d. The church recognized the divine authority of the canonical books.

2. Which of the following was one of the last books to be considered part of the canon?
   a. 3 John
   b. Hebrews
   c. Romans
   d. Mark

3. Approximately how many of the twenty-seven books of the New Testament were being functionally used as Scripture by the second century?
   a. Seven
   b. Eighteen
   c. Twenty-two
   d. Twenty-seven

4. Which of the definitions of canon looks at the canon from God's perspective?
   a. The exclusive definition
   b. The functional definition
   c. The ontological definition
   d. All of the above

5. According to theologian B.B. Warfield, the canon of the New Testament was complete by what year AD?
   a. 70
   b. 98
   c. 325
   d. 405

6. Dr. Kruger argues that the New Testament books were canon from the moment they were written by virtue of which of the following?
   a. Their Apostolic authorship
   b. Their divine inspiration
   c. Their doctrinal importance
   d. Their reception as Scripture by the early church

Answer Key—The Definition of Canon

REFLECTION & DISCUSSION QUESTIONS

Before the Video

What Do You Think?

These are personal questions. The answers should be based on your own knowledge and experience.

Scripture Reading

- What do these verses teach about the sacred nature of God's inspired words?

  These verses issue a grave warning to those who would make human additions or subtractions to God's inspired words. This prohibition indicates the finality and completion of God's revealed words; no edits or amendments are to be made. Moreover, it clearly delineates the distinction between the words of God and the words of man. It presupposes that God has instituted a distinct body of writings that is unique among all other written works.

During the Video

The Exclusive Definition of Canon

- According to the exclusive definition of canon, what determines the canonical status of a book?

  The exclusive definition of canon understands the canon as a fixed, final, and closed list of books. In this case, a book's canonical status is determined by whether it makes it into a final list of books that the church agrees on.

- How does holding the exclusive definition of canon affect the date that one assigns to the canon?

  If the New Testament canon is dated based on when a fixed, closed list of canonical books was formally adopted, then the canon dates to the fourth or fifth century. This is the approach to defining and dating canon that is most common among popular contemporary scholarship.

The Functional Definition of Canon

- According to the functional definition of canon, what determines the canonical status of a book?

  The functional definition of canon understands the canon as books that are used by Christians as Scripture. In this case, a book's canonical status is determined by whether the church has been reading it, preaching from it, studying it, and memorizing it as the Word of God.

- How does holding the functional definition of canon affect the date that one assigns to the canon?

  If the New Testament canon is dated based on when Christians had begun to use the New Testament books consistently as Scripture, then the canon dates to the second century. This approach to defining and dating canon suggests that the New Testament canon was functionally in place two hundred years before the dates proposed by critical scholars.

The Ontological Definition of Canon

- According to the ontological definition of canon, what determines the canonical status of a book?

  The ontological definition of canon understands the canon as the books that God gave to His church. In this case, a book's canonical status is confirmed by the sheer fact that it has come from God.

- How does holding the ontological definition of canon affect the date that one assigns to the canon?

  If the New Testament canon is dated based on when God gave these inspired documents to His church, then the canon dates to the first century. This approach to defining and dating canon recognizes that the New Testament canon was fully in place when John completed the book of Revelation around AD 98, even if the church did not begin using it as Scripture until the second century and did not agree on a fixed list until the fourth or fifth century.

After the Video

- Does an understanding of history lead to a definition of canon, or does a definition of canon lead to a particular understanding of history? Explain your answer.

  Many Christians assume that history is a set of neat and tidy facts that scholars use to form a scientific and objective definition of canon. However, the process of interpreting history is shaped significantly by the worldviews and assumptions about the canon that scholars already have. One's preconceived definition of canon determines how the historical evidence is interpreted. As a result, scholars who conceive of the canon simply as a list adopted by humans may wrongly conclude that Christians were wandering in the dark, functioning without a canon, until the fourth or fifth century.

- What are the strengths and weaknesses of each of the three definitions of canon?

  A strength of the exclusive definition of canon is that it reminds us that the development of the canon took time and was not complete until around the fourth century. One weakness of this definition is that it can contribute to the misconception that the church was operating in the dark until the fourth or fifth century. A second weakness of this definition is that it can create the mistaken impression that the church created the canon and that the canon is therefore of merely human origin. A strength of the functional definition of canon is that it balances the first definition by reminding us that the church was using nearly all of the New Testament writings as Scripture centuries before a fixed, closed list was agreed on. A shared weakness of the exclusive and functional definitions is that they do not address the ontology, or true essence, of a canonical book. The strength of the ontological definition is that it provides what is missing from the first two definitions by defining the canonical books first and foremost in terms of the fact that they were breathed out by God as gifts to His church. The canonical standing of the New Testament books is not determined by the church; it is determined by God and later recognized by His people.

- What is the big picture of the canon's development that these three definitions form when considered together?

The exclusive, functional, and ontological definitions complement one another to present a balanced picture of the formation of the New Testament canon. The canon began with God, who gave inspired books to His church throughout the first century. By the second century, the church began to use these inspired books as Scripture. By the fourth century, the church arrived at a full consensus regarding its formal recognition of the twenty-seven inspired books that had already been functioning as Scripture in the lives of Christians for centuries.

REVIEW QUIZ

Lesson 2

1. **D.**

   God is the source of the canon. The church's primary role in the formation of the canon was to recognize and affirm the inspiration and divine authority that the canonical books already possessed.

2. **A.**

   The four Gospels and the writings of Paul were among the earliest New Testament books to be considered canonical by the church. The book of 3 John, along with shorter General Epistles like 2 Peter, 2 John, and Jude, took longer than most to be universally recognized as Scripture by the church.

3. **C.**

   Contrary to the popular misconception that the church was wandering in the dark until the adoption of the canon in the fourth or fifth century, about twenty-two of the twenty-seven New Testament books were already being consistently used as Scripture by the second century.

4. **C.**

   The exclusive definition and functional definition both view the canon from the perspective of when people began to acknowledge and receive the books of the New

Testament as canonical. In contrast, the ontological definition views the canon from the perspective of God's act of inspiring and giving them to His church, even before their canonical status was recognized.

5. **B.**

    Writing on the topic of the New Testament canon in 1892, Princeton theologian B.B. Warfield stated, "The canon of the New Testament was completed when the last authoritative book was given to any church by the apostles, and that was when John wrote the Apocalypse, about A.D. 98."

6. **B.**

    Dr. Kruger observes that the New Testament writings were canon from the moment they were written by virtue of their divine inspiration. This statement reflects the reality that Scripture's status and authority come from God alone.

3

The Reason for Canon

INTRODUCTION

Critical scholars have popularized the idea that the canon was arbitrarily imposed on Christians in an effort to elevate one form of Christianity above others. Popular as this view has become, it has no historical warrant. In this lecture, Dr. Kruger presents several theological beliefs of the early church that would have naturally and organically led to the formation and adoption of the New Testament canon.

LEARNING GOALS

When you have finished this lesson, you should be able to:
- Differentiate between two distinct models for the reception of the New Testament canon
- Articulate three doctrinal beliefs of the early church that would have facilitated the reception of the New Testament canon

KEY IDEAS

- Early Christians believed that Jesus had completed the story of the Old Testament.
- Early Christians believed that Jesus had started a new covenant, which would be accompanied by written covenant documents.
- Early Christians believed that the Apostles and their writings spoke with the authority of the Lord Jesus Christ.

REFLECTION & DISCUSSION QUESTIONS

Before the Video

What Do You Think?

> Take a moment to answer the following questions. They will prepare you for the lecture.
>
> - Is it necessary for Christians to have a canon? Why or why not?
>
> - Do you think the Apostles and the early followers of Jesus Christ would have considered themselves to be part of a new religion? Explain your answer.

Scripture Reading

> *And we have the prophetic word more fully confirmed, to which you will do well to pay attention as to a lamp shining in a dark place, until the day dawns and the morning star rises in your hearts, knowing this first of all, that no prophecy of Scripture comes from someone's own interpretation. For no prophecy was ever produced by the will of man, but men spoke from God as they were carried along by the Holy Spirit.*
>
> —2 Peter 1:19–21
>
> - According to these verses, is the canon of divine or human origin? Explain your answer.

During the Video

> Answer the following questions while you watch the video. They will guide you through the lecture.

Continuity with the Old Testament   *0:00–12:46*

- What are the two competing paradigms about the New Testament canon?

- What are some of the promises that God made to His people in the Old Testament?

- What New Testament passages suggest that first-century Jews were expecting God to finish the Old Testament's story?

A New Covenant   12:46–17:13

- What evidence from the New Testament indicates that early Christians interpreted the work of Jesus within a covenantal framework?

- Which Old Testament passages demonstrate the link between covenants and written books?

Apostolic Authority   17:13–23:02

- What were the main features of the Apostles' role in the early church?

- What do 2 Thessalonians 2:15 and 3:14 indicate about the authority of Apostolic writings in the early church?

After the Video

Answer the following questions after you have finished the lecture. They will help you identify and summarize the major points.

- How are the genealogies in Chronicles and Matthew significant to the study of canon?

  If you are in a group, have the members discuss portions of Scripture that have been a challenge for them to read and study. How might God use these less popular portions of His Word to communicate important truths?

- Do the three doctrinal convictions discussed in this lecture need to be true in order to be significant to the study of canon? Why or why not?

  If you are in a group, have the members discuss which of these three beliefs they consider to be most compelling to their understanding of the formation of the canon.

- How was the metaphor of a plant used to contrast the two differing views of canon? Which view do you find more persuasive?

  If you are in a group, have the members discuss what they consider to be the most important or helpful aspects of Dr. Kruger's lectures on the New Testament canon so far.

PRAYER

Commit what you have learned in this lesson to prayer.

- Praise God for sending Jesus to complete the incomplete story of the Old Testament.
- Confess a specific way that you have broken God's covenant and need His forgiveness.
- Thank God for giving you His Word as an authority in your life.
- Ask God to give you an increased hunger for His Word.

REVIEW QUIZ

Use these multiple-choice questions to measure what you learned from this lesson.

1. Dr. Kruger believes that most first-century Christians would have been surprised to learn that a New Testament canon exists today.
   a. True
   b. False

2. Which metaphor most accurately represents the development of the New Testament canon?
   a. A diverse garden weeded down over time until a single plant remained
   b. A foreign plant abruptly transplanted into the soil of early Christianity
   c. A seed organically growing to maturity in the soil of early Christianity
   d. A tree requiring consistent pruning by various church councils

3. Which of the following best describes the overarching story of the Hebrew Bible?
   a. A metaphor for the human spiritual condition
   b. A story in search of a conclusion
   c. A story with a happy ending
   d. A story without a purpose

4. Which of the following books is believed to have occupied the final place in the order of the ancient Old Testament canon?
   a. Chronicles
   b. Esther
   c. Malachi
   d. Nehemiah

5. According to Dr. Kruger, which of the following best describes the role of a covenant in the ancient world?
   a. Business contract
   b. Neutrality pact
   c. Holy law
   d. Treaty

6. Which of the following was *not* presented as an argument why a written canon would have been a natural idea within the intellectual framework of early Christianity?
   a. The unfinished nature of the Old Testament
   b. The unfolding revelation of the Trinitarian nature of God
   c. The inauguration of a new covenant and the precedent of written covenant documents in the old covenant
   d. The understanding that Apostolic documents held binding authority

Answer Key—The Reason for Canon

Before the Video

What Do You Think?

> *These are personal questions. The answers should be based on your own knowledge and experience.*

Scripture Reading

- According to these verses, is the canon of divine or human origin? Explain your answer.

  In this passage, Peter rejects the idea that Scripture is of merely human origin. Rather, he affirms that Scripture is both a divine and a human document. Human authors who "were carried along by the Holy Spirit" spoke from God. Consequently, the Bible bears the unique imprint of both its divine and human authors. It speaks poignantly to the human condition and authentically resonates with the experiences of its human readers while also speaking with an authority and perspective that transcend all other human literary endeavors.

During the Video

Continuity with the Old Testament

- What are the two competing paradigms about the New Testament canon?

  Critical scholarship espouses the paradigm that the early church was not interested in a written canon, and that the canon was a later invention that was foisted on the church. Dr. Kruger argues for a different paradigm, that the emergence of the canon would have been a natural, logical, and inevitable development in early Christianity.

- What are some of the promises that God made to His people in the Old Testament?

  Dr. Kruger summarized the promises of God in the Old Testament as follows: God promised to redeem a people for Himself. He promised to save them, to forgive their sins, and to usher in His kingdom through His Messiah. God promised to break into the world in an amazing way to transform it and redeem it. These promises are consistently displayed throughout the Old Testament, but the Old Testament comes to an end before these promises are fulfilled.

- What New Testament passages suggest that first-century Jews were expecting God to finish the Old Testament's story?

John 1:41 indicates that people were looking for the Messiah. Luke 2:38 mentions that people were waiting for the redemption of Jerusalem. Luke 2:25 reports that Simeon was longing for the consolation of Israel. Acts 1:6 alludes to the general expectation that God was going to restore the kingdom of Israel. Jesus' announcement in Mark 1:15 that the kingdom of God was at hand is consistent with the general mood of expectation among first-century Jews that God would one day finish the story that He had begun in the Old Testament.

A New Covenant

- What evidence from the New Testament indicates that early Christians interpreted the work of Jesus in a covenantal framework?

  During the Last Supper, Jesus presented His imminent death in a covenantal framework by stating that He was inaugurating a new covenant sealed in His blood. In Luke 1:72, Zechariah anticipated the coming of Christ in terms of God remembering His holy covenant to Israel. In 2 Corinthians 3:6, Paul describes himself as a minister of the new covenant. Additionally, the book of Hebrews makes various references to a new covenant, mentioning Jesus as its guarantor and Christians as its beneficiaries.

- Which Old Testament passages demonstrate the link between covenants and written books?

  Exodus 24:7 and 2 Kings 23:2 specifically refer to "the Book of the Covenant." Deuteronomy 4:13 and Exodus 34:28 describe the Ten Commandments, written on stone tablets, as God's covenant. Deuteronomy 29:21 refers to "the covenant written in this Book of the Law." These verses indicate that in the minds of the Jewish people, a close link existed between God's covenant and written words. It is therefore to be expected that first-century Jews would naturally anticipate the arrival of new written documents to authenticate and bear witness to the new covenant in Christ.

Apostolic Authority

- What were the main features of the Apostles' role in the early church?

  The New Testament reveals that Jesus appointed the Apostles to serve as special representatives to bear His authority in a unique way. Not only could these Apostles perform signs and miracles, but also, when they spoke, Christ spoke. When they acted, Christ acted. In this context, the words that an Apostle spoke in the performance of his Apostolic office were considered to be as authoritative as the words of Christ.

- What do 2 Thessalonians 2:15 and 3:14 indicate about the authority of Apostolic writings in the early church?

  In 2 Thessalonians 2:15, Paul urges believers to hold on to the teachings that he and the other Apostles had communicated in both their spoken words and written letters. Paul wanted the Thessalonian church to understand that both his verbal and written instructions bore the same authority, that of Christ. For this reason, 2 Thessalonians 3:14 directs the church to apply corrective discipline to those who do not obey the instructions contained in Paul's letters. This command implies that the written words of the Apostles carried the same authority as the spoken words of Jesus.

After the Video

- How are the genealogies in Chronicles and Matthew significant to the study of canon?

  The book of Chronicles, which begins with a detailed genealogy, was arranged as the final book in the Old Testament canon in the Hebrew Bible. The gospel of Matthew, which also begins with a genealogy, is the first book in the New Testament canon. By beginning his account with a genealogy of Jesus, Matthew is establishing a symbolic link between his account and the unfinished story of the Old Testament. He is suggesting that the life and work of Jesus, described in his gospel, picks up where the book of Chronicles left off.

- Do the three doctrinal convictions discussed in this lecture need to be true in order to be significant to the study of canon? Why or why not?

  Dr. Kruger points out that for the purposes of understanding the formation of canon, the three convictions shared by first-century Christians do not technically need to be true in order to demonstrate that the emergence of a new canon was consistent with the beliefs and expectations of the Christian community at that time. Nevertheless, these three doctrinal convictions are true and faithful expressions of biblical teaching.

- How was the metaphor of a plant used to contrast the two differing views of canon? Which view do you find more persuasive?

  Dr. Kruger suggests that the New Testament canon was like a seed that was placed in the soil of early Christianity from the very beginning. Over time, this seed sprouted and grew to the point where it reached full maturity several centuries later. On the other hand, critical scholarship envisions a scenario in which the church abruptly excavated and disrupted the soil of early Christianity in the fifth century in order to transplant a foreign organism that previously had no place in the lives of Christians.

REVIEW QUIZ

Lesson 3

1. **B.**

   Critical scholars have presented the theory that early Christians would have considered a New Testament canon unnecessary and unexpected. However, Dr. Kruger presents evidence in this lecture to suggest that the idea of a canon would have been quite natural and even necessary in the minds of first-century Christians.

2. **C.**

   The theological context of first-century Judaism provided all the nutrients in the soil of early Christianity for the idea and reality of the New Testament canon to emerge gradually over time, as a seed that was present from the beginning and gradually grows to maturity.

3. **B.**

   A contemporary scholar has noted that "the great story of the Hebrew scriptures was therefore inevitably read . . . as a story in search of a conclusion."

4. **A.**

   The book of Chronicles, which was originally a single book instead of two separate books, is the last book in the Hebrew Bible. Experts believe that the order of books has not changed in the Hebrew Bible over the last two thousand years, meaning that Chronicles marked the end of the Old Testament at the time of Christ.

5. **D.**

   It is most helpful to think of a covenant as a form of ancient treaty between two parties. It was common in the ancient world for rulers to formalize diplomatic relations between their nations in the form of covenant treaties that were binding on both parties.

6. **B.**

   Based on the unfinished nature of the Old Testament, the inauguration of a new covenant with the precedent of written covenant documents, and the understanding that Apostolic documents held binding authority, Dr. Kruger presents a strong case in this lecture that the emergence of a new canon would have fit comfortably within the first-century Christian mind-set.

4

The Date of the Canon

INTRODUCTION

Throughout this series, Dr. Kruger has critiqued the prevalent belief that the New Testament canon was invented by the church in the fourth or fifth century. But when did the books of the New Testament start being used as Scripture? In this lesson, Dr. Kruger examines the history of the early church, uncovering substantial evidence that the believers from the period of the New Testament onward were consistently reading, teaching, and relying on the core of the New Testament canon as the Word of God.

LEARNING GOALS

When you have finished this lesson, you should be able to:

- Cite the names of several Christian leaders from the first three centuries of the church who interacted with the books of the New Testament as canonical
- Identify the books that served as an early canonical core of the New Testament

KEY IDEAS

- Irenaeus' use of a canon in the late second century was not unique among the church fathers.
- A robust body of witnesses confirms that New Testament books were used as Scripture in the early second century.
- The writings of Peter and Paul clearly suggest that the very first generation of believers considered New Testament writings to be the Word of God.

REFLECTION & DISCUSSION QUESTIONS

Before the Video

What Do You Think?

Take a moment to answer the following questions. They will prepare you for the lecture.

- What comes to your mind when you think of the history of the church in the first two centuries after Christ?

- The books of the Bible that we read today have been read and cherished by believers across the centuries. How can an awareness of the Bible's impact throughout history enrich your relationship with God's Word?

Scripture Reading

And count the patience of our Lord as salvation, just as our beloved brother Paul also wrote to you according to the wisdom given him, as he does in all his letters when he speaks in them of these matters. There are some things in them that are hard to understand, which the ignorant and unstable twist to their own destruction, as they do the other Scriptures.

—2 Peter 3:15–16

- What does Peter say about Paul's letters? Why is this significant?

During the Video

Answer the following questions while you watch the video. They will guide you through the lecture.

The Witness of Irenaeus and His Contemporaries   *0:00–11:04*

- What is the "big bang theory of canon"?

- Why is the document known as the Muratorian fragment significant to the study of canon?

The Witness of Irenaeus' Predecessors   *11:04–17:44*

- How did Justin Martyr describe a typical Christian worship service in the mid-second century? Why is this significant?

- What unique connection did Papias, bishop of Hierapolis, have to the New Testament writers?

The Witness of the Apostles   *17:44–22:30*

- To which two New Testament passages does Dr. Kruger refer? How do these passages inform our perspective on the early church's use of the New Testament?

After the Video

Answer the following questions after you have finished the lecture. They will help you identify and summarize the major points.

- How did Irenaeus' firm belief in the four Gospels shape his understanding of the very nature of creation? Why is his conviction about the four Gospels at odds with contemporary critical scholarship?

    If you are in a group, have the members share examples of how their faith has changed the way that they see the world. In what ways might the worldviews of critical scholars be shaping the way that they see the history of the early church?

- Does the evidence from Irenaeus' contemporaries and predecessors suggest that Irenaeus invented the canon? Why or why not?

    If you are in a group, have the members identify a Christian leader mentioned in this lecture of whom they had not heard before. How could a greater awareness of church history benefit Christians today?

- The New Testament contains multiple instances of one Apostle confirming that another Apostle's writings are God's Word. What does this teach us about the early church? How can this strengthen our confidence in God's Word?

If you are in a group, have the members read and discuss Jesus' words in John 17:22–23. In what ways can Christian unity advance the cause of Christ? Share examples of times you have seen Christians demonstrate the unity of Christ well to those around them.

PRAYER

Commit what you have learned in this lesson to prayer.

- Praise God for instilling a rich love for His Word in the hearts of His people centuries ago.
- Confess times when it has been difficult for you to love and embrace God's Word.
- Thank God for the faithful witness of the many generations of Christians who have gone before you.
- Ask God to help you teach others to love and obey His Word.

REVIEW QUIZ

Use these multiple-choice questions to measure what you learned from this lesson.

1. Who or which of the following was *not* from the same time period as Irenaeus?
   a. Clement of Alexandria
   b. Papias of Hierapolis
   c. Theophilus of Antioch
   d. The Muratorian fragment

2. In his apologetic treatise *To Autolycus*, Theophilus of Antioch primarily argued for which of the following?
   a. The canonicity of twenty-two of the twenty-seven New Testament books
   b. The equal authority of the Old and New Testaments
   c. The heretical nature of the Gospel of Thomas
   d. The lack of need for a formal canon

3. Which second-century Christian leader noted that he used the same books that had been handed down from the Apostles?
   a. Clement of Alexandria
   b. Irenaeus of Lyon
   c. Justin Martyr
   d. Theophilus of Antioch

4. Which church father used the phrase "Memoirs of the Apostles" to refer to the Gospels?
   a. Ignatius of Antioch
   b. Irenaeus of Lyon
   c. Justin Martyr
   d. Papias of Hierapolis

5. In his writings, Papias, the second-century bishop of Hierapolis, mentioned interacting with which New Testament figure?
   a. Barnabas
   b. John
   c. Mark
   d. Timothy

6. In 1 Timothy 5:18, Paul uses the term *scripture* to describe the words of which New Testament author?
   a. James
   b. John
   c. Luke
   d. Peter

Answer Key—The Date of the Canon

REFLECTION & DISCUSSION QUESTIONS

Before the Video

What Do You Think?

> *These are personal questions. The answers should be based on your own knowledge and experience.*

Scripture Reading

- What does Peter say about Paul's letters? Why is this significant?

> *Peter's act of comparing Paul's writings to "the other Scriptures" is clear evidence that he considered the letters of Paul to be Scripture. This is significant because it reveals, in opposition to the views of critical scholars, that the designation of the New Testament writings as Scripture took place in the first century, not centuries later. Additionally, Peter's statement that some things in Paul's letters are hard to understand can be a source of consolation to believers who struggle to understand parts of God's Word.*

During the Video

The Witness of Irenaeus and His Contemporaries

- What is the "big bang theory of canon"?

> *The "big bang theory of canon" is the idea that the canon emerged suddenly. This theory identifies Irenaeus of Lyon as the innovator who first pioneered the use of a canon at a time when nothing like it had been used before. Dr. Kruger finds this theory to be problematic and instead argues for a much more gradual model of canonical development.*

- Why is the document known as the Muratorian fragment significant to the study of canon?

> *The Muratorian fragment is the remaining portion of an ancient manuscript dating from the late second century. It is significant because it was written independently of Irenaeus but nevertheless lists essentially the same books that Irenaeus considered canonical. Consequently, this manuscript confirms that other Christians living at the time of Irenaeus already held the same views on the canon.*

The Witness of Irenaeus' Predecessors

- How did Justin Martyr describe a typical Christian worship service in the mid-second century? Why is this significant?

Writing around AD 150, Justin Martyr records that all of the Christians in an area would gather on Sunday. Someone would read from one of the Gospels and from the Old Testament as long as time permitted. Afterward, the leader of the assembly would offer verbal instruction and exhortation to the congregation. This description indicates not only that second-century believers considered the Gospels to hold equal authority to the Old Testament but also that the basic format of Christian worship has not changed fundamentally in 1,800 years.

- What unique connection did Papias, bishop of Hierapolis, have to the New Testament writers?

   Writing in the early second century, Papias records that he received instruction from someone known as "the Elder." Evidence suggests that "the Elder" refers to the Apostle John, who wrote a gospel, three epistles, and the book of Revelation. This connection to John gave Papias a unique perspective on the composition, authorship, and authority of the New Testament writings.

The Witness of the Apostles

- To which two New Testament passages does Dr. Kruger refer? How do these passages inform our perspective on the early church's use of the New Testament?

   Dr. Kruger refers to 2 Peter 3:16 and 1 Timothy 5:18. In 2 Peter 3:16, Peter refers to the letters of Paul as "scripture." This suggests not only that he believed them to be inspired by God, but that his readers in the first century were already familiar with a body of Pauline writings. In 1 Timothy 5:18, Paul cites Luke 10:7 and refers to it as "scripture." This demonstrates Paul's familiarity with the gospel of Luke, which he evidently considered to be the Word of God.

After the Video

- How did Irenaeus' firm belief in the four Gospels shape his understanding of the nature of creation? Why is his conviction about the four Gospels at odds with contemporary critical scholarship?

   Irenaeus considered the fourfold Gospels of Matthew, Mark, Luke, and John to be so certain and established that he began to see the number four as being built into the fabric of creation. He cited the four directions of the compass and the four faces of the angelic beings around the throne in Revelation as evidence that four is a number of perfection and completeness. Irenaeus' passionate advocacy for the finality of the four Gospels undermines the claims of critical scholars that Matthew, Mark, Luke, and John were simply a few writings taken from a larger pool of equally authoritative gospel accounts that were later abandoned.

- Does the evidence from Irenaeus' contemporaries and predecessors suggest that Irenaeus invented the canon? Why or why not?

The evidence presented in this lesson demonstrates that Irenaeus' views on the canon reflect a consensus that was already beginning to form among Christian leaders generations earlier. In fact, the roots of this canonical consensus can be seen as early as the first-century writings of Peter and Paul.

- The New Testament contains multiple instances of one Apostle confirming that another Apostle's writings are in fact God's Word. What does this teach us about the early church? How can this strengthen our confidence in God's Word?

The Apostolic endorsements of one another's writings indicate many things. First, these statements show that the Apostles were aware of one another's writings and were reading them. Additionally, these statements reveal a spirit of unity among the Apostles. Moreover, statements like Peter's testimony about Paul's letters and Paul's affirmation of Luke's gospel are precisely what one would expect to see in a collection of divinely inspired books. The Spirit who inspired the composition of the New Testament worked through a diverse array of human authors to produce a collection of writings that is coherent, unified, and trustworthy.

REVIEW QUIZ

Lesson 4

1. **B.**
   Clement of Alexandria, Theophilus of Antioch, and the Muratorian fragment are all from the late second century, and they all affirm a canon very similar to Irenaeus' canon. Papias of Hierapolis, who lived in the first half of the second century, considered the majority of the books in Irenaeus' canon to be Scripture as well.

2. **B.**
   While presenting the case for Christianity to Autolycus, Theophilus of Antioch argued that the New Testament writings were as authoritative as the Old Testament. As a contemporary of Irenaeus, Theophilus is another source of evidence that the New Testament was considered to be Scripture in the second century and that Irenaeus didn't create the idea of the New Testament canon.

3. **A.**
   In describing the books that he considered canonical, Clement of Alexandria commented that those books were the ones that had been handed down to the church from the Apostles. Clement, therefore, perceived that these books had always had a special place in the life of the church.

4. **C.**
   Justin Martyr famously referred to Matthew, Mark, Luke, and John as the "Memoirs of the Apostles," a phrase that affirms their Apostolic origins, their eyewitness credibility, and their longstanding use in the church.

5. **B.**

   Papias of Hierapolis mentioned in his writings that he had personally received instruction from a teacher known as "the Elder." Evidence suggests that "the Elder" was the Apostle John.

6. **C.**

   In 1 Timothy 5:18, Paul quotes two different passages as Scripture. One quotation comes from the book of Deuteronomy, and the other quotation comes from the gospel of Luke.

5

The Authors of the Canon

INTRODUCTION

Having made a thorough case for an early and gradual process of canon formation, Dr. Kruger now turns his attention to the authorship of the New Testament. In this lecture, he will examine and critique a misconception about New Testament authorship that is rampant in both Christian and secular circles. As Dr. Kruger points out, a correct understanding of the intention of the authors of the New Testament can help us avoid common and deadly errors in our approach to God's Word.

LEARNING GOALS

When you have finished this lesson, you should be able to:

- Explain the significance of the awareness of the New Testament authors that God was breathing out His Word through them for the sake of His church
- Trace the theme of authoritative Apostolic teaching throughout the New Testament

KEY IDEAS

- The authors of the New Testament had a clear sense that they were writing God's words to His people.
- A correct understanding of Apostolic authority leads to a correct perspective on the canonical process and the authority of God's Word.
- The theme of authoritative Apostolic teaching can be clearly seen throughout the New Testament canon.

REFLECTION & DISCUSSION QUESTIONS

Before the Video

What Do You Think?

Take a moment to answer the following questions. They will prepare you for the lecture.

- What is your first memory of reading God's Word? How have your interactions with Scripture changed since then?

- Do you think the authors of the New Testament were aware at the time that they were recording Scripture? Do you think the original readers knew that they were reading Scripture? Why or why not?

Scripture Reading

And we also thank God constantly for this, that when you received the word of God, which you heard from us, you accepted it not as the word of men but as what it really is, the word of God, which is at work in you believers.

—1 Thessalonians 2:13

- How did the Christians in Thessalonica receive Paul's teaching? What does this imply about the formation of the New Testament canon?

During the Video

Answer the following questions while you watch the video. They will guide you through the lecture.

Authoritative Apostolic Teaching in Paul's Letters   *0:00–13:23*

- How does Paul describe his Apostolic authority in the first chapter of his letter to the Galatians? On the basis of this authority, what clear warning does he issue to them?

- How does Paul describe the authority of his words and the implications of rejecting them in 1 Corinthians 14:37–38?

Authoritative Apostolic Teaching in the Gospels   *13:23–18:15*

- What role does the "beloved disciple" play in the gospel of John? Why is this significant?

- Why is it appropriate to think of Luke's gospel as an Apostolic book?

Authoritative Apostolic Teaching in Hebrews and Revelation   *18:15–22:52*

- How does the unnamed author of Hebrews affirm his Apostolic credentials?

- How do the beginning and end of Revelation convey John's conviction that he was recording the Word of God?

After the Video

Answer the following questions after you have finished the lecture. They will help you identify and summarize the major points.

- What widespread misconception about the authors of the New Testament is addressed in this lesson?

  If you are in a group, have the members discuss the extent to which they have personally encountered this common misconception—whether in a conversation, in sermons or teaching, or in their own thinking.

- How does the common misunderstanding discussed in this lesson affect one's approach to dating the New Testament canon?

  If you are in a group, have the members share how their thinking on the process of dating the canon has changed, has deepened, or has been challenged over the course of this teaching series.

- According to Dr. Kruger, why is it theologically dangerous to conclude that the New Testament books became Scripture over time?

  If you are in a group, have the members answer this question: What practical difference does it make whether the church's authority comes from the Bible or the Bible's authority comes from the church?

PRAYER

Commit what you have learned in this lesson to prayer.

- Praise God for providing His Word as the authority for faith and life.
- Confess specific ways that you have resisted God's authority in your life.
- Thank God for calling you to a life of holiness and for shepherding you by His Word.
- Ask God to make you humbly dependent on Him in a specific area of your life.

REVIEW QUIZ

Use these multiple-choice questions to measure what you learned from this lesson.

1. "The authors of our New Testament books did not know they were writing scripture." Which of the following scholars made this bold claim?
   a. N.T. Wright
   b. Bart Ehrman
   c. Mark Allan Powell
   d. Walter Bauer

2. How did the New Testament authors most frequently indicate their awareness that they were writing Scripture?
   a. By explicitly claiming to be writing Scripture
   b. By citing the miraculous signs and wonders they had performed
   c. By affirming themselves to be one of the twelve original disciples
   d. By asserting that they were passing along authoritative Apostolic teaching

3. How many books did Paul contribute to the New Testament canon?
   a. Seven
   b. Ten
   c. Thirteen
   d. Fifteen

4. To which group of Christians did Paul most vividly articulate his claim to Apostolic authority by referring to his writing as a "command from the Lord"?
   a. The Corinthians
   b. The Galatians
   c. The Philippians
   d. The Thessalonians

5. Of which New Testament writer do even non-Christian scholars acknowledge that he considered his writings to be the natural continuation of the Old Testament narrative?
    a. John
    b. Luke
    c. Mark
    d. Matthew

6. Some first-century writings carried Apostolic authority even without direct Apostolic authorship.
    a. True
    b. False

Answer Key—The Authors of the Canon

REFLECTION & DISCUSSION QUESTIONS

Before the Video

What Do You Think?

> These are personal questions. The answers should be based on your own knowledge and experience.

Scripture Reading

- How did the Christians in Thessalonica receive Paul's teaching? What does this imply about the formation of the New Testament canon?

  Paul recalls that the Thessalonians received his words as if they were the Word of God and not merely human words. This indicates that the authors and recipients of New Testament texts recognized from the beginning that these writings were divinely inspired.

During the Video

Authoritative Apostolic Teaching in Paul's Letters

- How does Paul describe his Apostolic authority in the first chapter of his letter to the Galatians? On the basis of this authority, what clear warning does he issue to them?

  In Galatians 1:1, Paul vividly describes his Apostolic calling in terms of a direct mandate from Jesus Christ, rather than a status conferred on him by another human being. Having established his authority, Paul confronts the Galatians with the weighty accusation of having abandoned the gospel message (v. 6). He makes it clear that the message that they have forsaken came not just from him but from a revelation of Jesus Christ (vv. 11–12). Consequently, his rebuke to the Galatians is also a rebuke from Christ and an invitation to return to the true gospel.

- How does Paul describe the authority of his words and the implications of rejecting them in 1 Corinthians 14:37–38?

  In 1 Corinthians 14:37–38, Paul notes that the most spiritually discerning among his readers will acknowledge that his instructions to the Corinthian church are actually "the command of the Lord." On the basis of this authority, Paul goes on to write that anyone who does not recognize his authority to speak for Christ is in turn not to be recognized as a follower of Christ.

Authoritative Apostolic Teaching in the Gospels

- What role does the "beloved disciple" play in the gospel of John? Why is this significant?

  The "beloved disciple" makes numerous appearances at key moments in the gospel of John. He was present at the Last Supper, during which he reclined next to Jesus (13:23). He was also present when Peter was informed of specific details concerning his death (21:20). He was also present at the crucifixion (19:26) and went with Peter to the empty tomb (20:2). In the final words of John's gospel, it is revealed that this "beloved disciple" is in fact the author of this account of Jesus' life (21:24). As an active observer of so many key events in the life of Jesus, John is a valuable source of information about Jesus that is not available in any of the other three Gospels.

- Why is it appropriate to think of Luke's gospel as an Apostolic book?

  Even though Luke was not one of the twelve Apostles, he occupied an important place in the Apostolic circle by virtue of his role as Paul's traveling companion. He made painstaking efforts to learn from the Apostles and record their eyewitness testimony concerning the life of Jesus. In the prologue to his gospel, Luke emphasizes the fact that his account of Jesus' life is a carefully documented presentation of the Apostolic witness concerning Christ (1:2–3).

Authoritative Apostolic Teaching in Hebrews and Revelation

- How does the unnamed author of Hebrews affirm his Apostolic credentials?

  Although the author of the book of Hebrews does not reveal his identity, he makes no secret of the fact that he has gotten his information directly from those who had received teaching firsthand from Jesus and whose authority to minister in His name had been confirmed by miraculous signs (2:3–4). Therefore, though the author himself may not have been an Apostle, his teaching came directly from Apostolic sources.

- How do the beginning and end of Revelation convey John's conviction that he was recording the Word of God?

  John begins Revelation with a clear and direct statement that its contents are not his own invention but are instead a "revelation of Jesus Christ" (1:1). He concludes the book with a severe warning not to add or subtract anything from this book (22:18–19). His statement that God Himself would punish those who would alter the inspired words indicates that the weight of divine authority rests on what John has written.

After the Video

- What widespread misconception about the authors of the New Testament is addressed in this lesson?

In this lesson, Dr. Kruger confronted the common assumption that the authors of the New Testament writings did not intend to write Scripture and were unaware that the Holy Spirit was working through them to give His Word to the church. According to this model of inspiration, these books would have been considered fairly ordinary when they were written and were only gradually recognized to have been divinely inspired.

- How does the common misunderstanding discussed in this lesson affect one's approach to dating the New Testament canon?

  The common misconception that the New Testament authors were unaware that they were writing Scripture implies a lengthy gap of time between the composition of the New Testament books and their inclusion in the canon. According to this model, it could have taken several generations for these books to gain the following needed to elevate them to canonical status. On the other hand, if they were considered to be the Word of God as soon as they were written, then the New Testament writings would have functioned as canonical Scripture right away.

- According to Dr. Kruger, why is it theologically dangerous to conclude that the New Testament books became Scripture over time?

  Dr. Kruger pointed out that any claim that the New Testament was not originally intended to be Scripture implies that the New Testament books became Scripture over time. This line of thinking suggests that the church has the power to grant scriptural status to writings that it considers important. The unfortunate result of this reasoning is that it leads to the conclusion that the church has authority over the Bible. Instead, the Bible's authority comes from God alone.

REVIEW QUIZ

Lesson 5

1. **C.**

   In his textbook Introducing the New Testament, *contemporary scholar Mark Allan Powell writes, "The authors of our New Testament books did not know they were writing scripture." Dr. Kruger cites this statement as evidence of how widespread this view has become.*

2. **D.**

   The most natural and consistent way for the writers of the New Testament to demonstrate the divine authority behind their words was by indicating that their writings were relating authoritative Apostolic teaching. Because Christ had given His authority to the Apostles, any claim to be presenting Apostolic teaching was in effect a claim to be speaking on Christ's behalf.

3. **C.**

   Paul wrote numerous letters to individuals and churches throughout the Mediterranean world, thirteen of which have a place in the New Testament canon. These inspired writings are the books of Romans, 1 and 2 Corinthians, Galatians, Ephesians, Philippians, Colossians, 1 and 2 Thessalonians, 1 and 2 Timothy, Titus, and Philemon.

4. **A.**

   Perhaps more than anywhere else, Paul plainly states his understanding of the Apostolic authority of his writing in 1 Corinthians 14:37, where he equates his writing with a "command from the Lord." Paul also recounts the events of his Apostolic calling and credentials in Galatians 1:1–2:10.

5. **D.**

   Matthew's gospel possesses a uniquely Jewish perspective and takes great pains to link itself to the inconclusive ending of the Hebrew canon. Matthew's self-awareness of continuing the Old Testament narrative is so apparent that even non-Christians scholars have taken note of it.

6. **A.**

   The books of Mark, Luke, Acts, and perhaps Hebrews were not written by Apostles. Nevertheless, they were based on teaching that the authors of these books had received firsthand from the Apostles themselves. Because they faithfully convey the testimony of the Apostles, these books have a valid claim to Apostolic authority.

6

The Attributes of the Canon

INTRODUCTION

A vast number of ancient writings claim to contain truth about the life and teachings of Jesus. For this reason, it is crucial for Christians to be able to offer clear reasons why some ancient writings have a place in the New Testament canon and why others do not. In this lesson, Dr. Kruger presents three distinguishing characteristics that set God's inspired books apart from all other human writings.

LEARNING GOALS

When you have finished this lesson, you should be able to:

- Identify and describe three essential attributes of canonical books
- Differentiate between inspired and noninspired ancient Christian texts
- Know with confidence that all the right books are a part of the New Testament canon

KEY IDEAS

- God has provided His church with the means to identify which books are from Him.
- Divinely inspired New Testament books have Apostolic origins, possess clear divine qualities, and enjoy the corporate reception of God's people.

REFLECTION & DISCUSSION QUESTIONS

Before the Video

What Do You Think?

Take a moment to answer the following questions. They will prepare you for the lecture.

- What makes reading the Bible different from reading any other book? How would you explain this difference to someone who has never read the Bible?

- Is it possible that a newly discovered book could be added to the New Testament canon today? Why or why not?

Scripture Reading

"If you are the Christ, tell us plainly." Jesus answered them, "I told you, and you do not believe. The works that I do in my Father's name bear witness about me, but you do not believe because you are not among my sheep. My sheep hear my voice, and I know them, and they follow me."

—John 10:24b–27

- What do these words of Jesus imply about the way His followers receive God's Word?

During the Video

Answer the following questions while you watch the video. They will guide you through the lecture.

Apostolic Origins   0:00–8:56

- What are the two ways that a book can have Apostolic origins?

- How strong is the Gospel of Thomas' claim to have Apostolic origins?

Divine Qualities   8:56–16:35

- What does it mean for a canonical book to demonstrate divine qualities?

- What are the three divine qualities of Scripture?

Corporate Reception   *16:35–22:36*

- What does it mean for canonical books to enjoy corporate reception?

- Why is the consensus of the church a reliable test of canonicity?

After the Video

Answer the following questions after you have finished the lecture. They will help you identify and summarize the major points.

- How is recognizing God's hand in creation similar to recognizing God's authorship of an inspired text?

If you are in a group, have the members describe memorable moments when they have encountered God through creation and through His Word.

- Why are the Bible's divine qualities not apparent to everyone who reads God's Word?

If you are in a group, have the members discuss the challenge of sharing God's Word with people who do not yet believe in Jesus. How can you help them grow in their awareness of the majesty of God's Word?

- Throughout this teaching series, Dr. Kruger has presented a broad array of biblical and historical evidence that supports the New Testament's claim to be the inspired and authoritative Word of God. How has this study informed your perspective on the New Testament canon? What unanswered questions do you still have?

If you are in a group, have the members share the most important things they have learned during this teaching series. How has God used this experience to deepen your relationship with Him?

PRAYER

Commit what you have learned in this lesson to prayer.

- Praise God for giving His people a reliable way to know which books are from Him.
- Confess times when you have not sufficiently witnessed to God's ability to speak through His Word.

- Thank God for giving you sixty-six trustworthy books to help you know and follow Him.
- Ask God to help you know His Word more fully and share it confidently.

REVIEW QUIZ

Use these multiple-choice questions to measure what you learned from this lesson.

1. How many apocryphal books can credibly be linked to the Apostles?
    a. Zero
    b. Three
    c. Seven
    d. Twelve

2. What prompted the second-century pagan philosopher Tatian to convert to Christianity?
    a. The beauty of the biblical narrative
    b. The courage displayed by heroic Christian martyrs
    c. The miraculous signs performed by ordinary Christians
    d. The power and efficacy of the Holy Spirit in the Bible

3. Approximately how many different human authors contributed to the Bible?
    a. 27
    b. 33
    c. 40
    d. 66

4. Despite its lack of Apostolic authorship, the Gospel of Thomas fits harmoniously with the Old Testament narrative.
    a. True
    b. False

5. Dr. Kruger suggests that the church's role in the formation of the canon is most similar to which of the following?
    a. A furnace
    b. A thermometer
    c. A thermostat
    d. An air duct

6. How did second- and third-century Christians regard the Gospel of Thomas?
    a. As a natural companion to the other four Gospels
    b. As a useful but uninspired teaching tool
    c. As heretical and deceptive
    d. As the inspired Word of God

Answer Key—The Attributes of the Canon

REFLECTION & DISCUSSION QUESTIONS

Before the Video

What Do You Think?

> *These are personal questions. The answers should be based on your own knowledge and experience.*

Scripture Reading

- What do these words of Jesus imply about the way His followers receive God's Word?

  Because Jesus Christ is God the Son, the written Word of God is also the Word of Jesus. When Jesus speaks through His Word, His sheep recognize and obey His voice. The New Testament is not considered to be the Word of God because the church declared it to be so; rather, the church considered the New Testament to be the Word of God because it recognized the voice of Jesus speaking through it and believed.

During the Video

Apostolic Origins

- What are the two ways that a book can have Apostolic origins?

  The first way that a book can qualify as having Apostolic origins is by being written directly by an Apostle. Most of the books in the New Testament canon fit this description. The second way that a book can have Apostolic origins is if it was written by a companion or friend of an Apostle who would have had access to reliable Apostolic testimony. Mark, Luke, Acts, and perhaps Hebrews fit in this category.

- How strong is the Gospel of Thomas' claim to have Apostolic origins?

  There is no evidence to suggest any direct connection to the Gospel of Thomas from the Apostles. Moreover, the Gospel of Thomas is a second-century document, written long after the death of Thomas and the other Apostles.

Divine Qualities

- What does it mean for a canonical book to demonstrate divine qualities?

  Books that are inspired by God possess certain characteristics that demonstrate their divine authorship. Even if we knew nothing about a book's origins, we could still conclude that a book has been inspired by God by detecting these signature marks.

- What are the three divine qualities of Scripture?

The first divine quality of Scripture is its beauty and excellency. The words of Scripture resonate with a dazzling elegance in which we can behold Christ Himself speaking to us. The second divine quality of Scripture is its power and authority. God's Word actively works in the hearts and minds of its readers to encourage, convict, rebuke, and instruct in a supernatural way. The third divine quality of Scripture is its unity and harmony. Acting under the inspiration of the Holy Spirit, the various writers of the sixty-six books of the Bible produced a narrative which seamlessly presents a coherent and compelling story of God's redemptive work in Jesus Christ.

Corporate Reception

- What does it mean for canonical books to enjoy corporate reception?

The corporate reception of the canon is the phenomenon by which every book given by God is recognized and received by God's people. When a large number of Christians agree that a book bears the marks of divine inspiration, that consensus is a strong indication that the book in question is in fact an inspired book.

- Why is the consensus of the church a reliable test of canonicity?

The consensus of the church is a reliable test of canonicity because the Holy Spirit is actively at work in His church to guide God's people to an accurate perception of the Word of God. The Spirit helps Christians to recognize and heed the voice of Christ (John 10:27) speaking through the inspired books that God has provided. In short, the testimony of the church can be trusted because the Spirit who guides the church can be trusted.

After the Video

- How is recognizing God's hand in creation similar to recognizing God's authorship of an inspired text?

God manifests His power through His creation (general revelation) and through His Word (special revelation) in a way that often speaks directly to human hearts. Just as a person who beholds the splendor of creation recognizes the power and majesty of its Creator, a person who reads God's Word can recognize the truth and power of its Author.

- Why are the Bible's divine qualities not apparent to everyone who reads God's Word?

Sadly, many people are unable to see the divine qualities of the Bible. In order to understand and appreciate the qualities of a living book, the person who is encountering the book must also be alive. Although the divine qualities of Scripture are fully and objectively present in God's Word, fallen people need God's Spirit to behold God's Word for what it truly is. Those who have received the Holy Spirit ought to ask the Spirit to open the eyes of others, that they might also behold the wonders of God's Word.

- Throughout this teaching series, Dr. Kruger has presented a broad array of biblical and historical evidence that supports the New Testament's claim to be the inspired and authoritative Word of God. How has this study informed your perspective on the New Testament canon? What unanswered questions do you still have?

  The answers to these questions should express what you consider to be the most significant aspects of your experience from this study and why. Consider ways that you can continue to explore the topic of this teaching series to deepen your relationship with Christ and help others have an increased confidence in His Word.

REVIEW QUIZ

Lesson 6

1. **A.**

   Of the many apocryphal writings that have been discovered from the early centuries of the Christian church, not one can be credibly linked to the Apostles. Only the twenty-seven books of the New Testament canon can claim first-century authorship and a clear, verifiable Apostolic connection.

2. **D.**

   The pagan philosopher Tatian famously converted to Christianity in the second century. His conversion was the result of his personal encounter with Scripture, through which he experienced the power and efficacy of the Spirit at work in God's Word.

3. **C.**

   The Bible was written by approximately forty distinct human authors. It demonstrates a supernatural unity and harmony due to its composition by a single divine Author.

4. **B.**

   The Gospel of Thomas is dramatically out of sync with the biblical narrative. It contains bizarre teachings, gnostic philosophy, and a variety of heresies. This lack of conformity with the Old Testament canon and the Apostolic writings is one of the reasons why the early church realized that the Gospel of Thomas was not divinely inspired.

5. **B.**

   Dr. Kruger compares the church's role in the canonical process to a thermometer, which measures and responds to the reality of the temperature, unlike a thermostat, heating system, or air duct, which all influence and alter the temperature. The church does not influence or change the status of divinely inspired books. It simply acknowledges and responds to the reality of what those books are.

6. **C.**

   Whenever the Gospel of Thomas is mentioned in the historical record, it receives consistent condemnation from the church fathers. It never appears on any lists of canonical or approved writings. The church viewed it as heretical and deceptive, altogether unworthy of inclusion in the canon.